ANOTHER GOOSE RHYME

BY
FLO ELLINGSEN

© 2002 by Flo Ellingsen.
All rights reserved.

No part of this book may be reproduced, stored in a retrieval system, or transmitted by any means, electronic, mechanical, photocopying, recording, or otherwise, without written permission from the author.

ISBN: 1-4033-5283-6

This book is printed on acid free paper.

1st Books - rev. 7/16/02

> **DEDICATED TO FRIENDLY FOLK
> CHERISHING
> MEMORIES OF CHILDHOOD**

My thanks for
excellent help
and encouragement to
Marjorie & Murle Menge
And
Barbara & John Abbott

A FOREWORD

If my Goose did lay an egg
   The color of pure gold,
      A tribute from the friendly folk
         To nonsense I have told.

Though my pockets could be bulging,
   My life would richer be.
      For giving pleasure to my friends,
     Is pleasure, too, for me.

Contents

1. Peter, Peter 1
2. Jack Be Nimble 3
3. Tickity, Tickity Tock 5
4. Hi-Diddle-Diddle 1 7
5. Ride A Cock-Horse 9
6. Henny Penny 11
7. Little Bo-Peep 13
8. Star Light 15
9. Little Miss Muffet 17
10. Georgie Porgie 19
11. Robin Red Breast 21
12. Little Boy Blue 23
13. King Arthur 25
14. Two Birds 27
15. Old Woman 29
16. St. Ives 31
17. Little Jack Horner 33
18. Goosey, Goosey, Gander 35
19. To Market, To Market 37
20. One Misty Moisty Morning 39
21. To Bed, To Bed 41
22. Rock-A-Bye Baby 43
23. Mary Had A Little Lamb 45
24. Pussy-Cat-Pussy Cat 47
25. Hi Diddle-Diddle - 2 49
26. Wee Willie Winkie 51
27. Mary, Mary 53
28. North Wind 55
29. This Little Pig 57

30.	Rub-A-Dub-Dub	59
31.	Little Jack Horner 2	61
32.	Cross Patch	63
33.	Jack And Jill	65
34.	Fishy, Fishy	67
35.	Oh Dear, Oh Dear	69
36.	See-Saw, See-Saw	71
37.	A Wise Man	73
38.	Sing A Song Of Sixpence	75
39.	Simple Simon 1	77
40.	Old Mother Hubbard	79
41.	God's Sparrow	81
42.	Twinkle, Twinkle, Little Star	83
43.	Humpty, Dumpty	85
44.	A Diller, A Dollar	87
45.	Jack Sprat	89
46.	Cock-A-Doodle-Doo	91
47.	Rain, Rain	93
48.	Simple Simon - 2	95
49.	Birdie, Birdie In The Tree,	97
50.	The Clock	99
51.	If Wishes Were Horses	101
52.	Rip-Van-Winkle	103
53.	At Night	105
54.	Three Blind Mice	107
55.	Old King Cole	109
56.	Hickity, Pickity	111
57.	Thirty Days Has September	113
58.	Ladybird	115
59.	I Saw A Ship A-Sailing	117
60.	Curly Locks	119
61.	Tweedle-Dee-Dee	121

62.	Lady From France	123
63.	The Lion And The Unicorn	125
64.	See A Pin	127
65.	Good Advice	129
66.	Hark, Hark	131
67.	All The Seas	133
68.	Good And Evil	135
69.	Bye Baby Bunting	137
70.	Hush-A-Bye Baby	139
71.	Polly	141
72.	Girls And Boys Come Out To Play	143
73.	Robin Hood	145
74.	Baa, Baa, Black Sheep	147
75.	Ten Little Toes	149

PETER, PETER

Peter, Peter told his wife
he'd like to change his diet.
But she advised him, "Peter, dear,
you hadn't better try it.

"Your health is good,
you'd better heed.
Some fats, I've heard,
are bad indeed."

Peter was a docile bumpkin,
so he agreed to eating pumpkin.

JACK BE NIMBLE

Jack be nimble, Jack be speedy,
you'll get more if you are greedy.
Jack be agile, Jack be fast,
or you'll end up being last.

TICKITY, TICKITY TOCK

Tickity, tickity, tock,
we have an electric clock.
If a mouse should get in,
it would short circuit him.
Tickity, tickity, tock.

Tickity, tickity, tock,
a mouse got into our clock.
He is gone from this world
but his hair is all curled.
Tickity, tickity, tock.

HI-DIDDLE-DIDDLE 1

Hi-diddle-diddle
recalls the tune
of the orbiting cow
who jumped over the moon.

The spectacular route
can be seen to this day.
It is commonly known
as the Milky Way.

RIDE A COCK-HORSE

Ride a Cock-Horse, whatever that means.
    Gallop or canter to places unseen.
Tommy has gone to market to buy
    bread and cake and an apple pie.

To portage these things is a problem, of course.
    It takes two hands to ride a Cock-Horse.
Tommy's solution was a matter of pride.
    Travel was simpler with the goodies inside.

HENNY PENNY

Henny Penny, the intrepid hen,
was joined by a duck and a goose.
This odd entourage must warn the king
that the sky had broken loose.

Henny Penny reportedly said,
"A piece of the sky just fell on my head."
The king bemused said, "You don't say;
I'll have someone fix it this very day."

LITTLE BO-PEEP

This is the tale of Little Bo-Peep.
 The story goes, she fell asleep
  and while asleep, she lost her sheep.

Alert on the job is a rule to heed.
 Behind is okay but it's better to lead.
  Luck also helps in your goal to succeed.

STAR LIGHT

Star Light, star bright,
first Satellite I see tonight.
    Circumnavigating earth,
      bouncing waves for all you're worth.

LITTLE MISS MUFFET

Little Miss Muffet
    secure on her tuffet,
        compulsively eating away.

It's not the big spider
    but hips getting wider
        that frightens Miss Muffet today.

GEORGIE PORGIE

Georgie Porgie kissed the girls
and then he ran away.
By george, it's still the same today
except that Georgie tries to stay.
You know he really isn't shy.
See that gleam in Georgie's eye?

ROBIN RED BREAST

Spring is surely on its way;
I saw my first Robin today.
There he was in all his glory
staking out his territory.

    Unlike the Warbler and the Thrush,
    he's early to avoid the rush.
    His beauty and his red, red breast
    sets him apart, he needs no crest.

        The early bird does get the worm.
        It is an old and much used term.
        But nature dictates, it's absurd,
        that worms are paté to this bird.

LITTLE BOY BLUE

Little Boy Blue, just like Bo-Peep,
  had a job to perform tending his sheep.
    Yet, in the middle of the day,
      Boy Blue decided to hit the hay.
        That is the reason, I've heard it said,
        his entire flock just up and fled.

KING ARTHUR

When good King Arthur ruled his land,
he used a firm but gentle hand.
His council sat at a table round,
where no one was allowed to pound.

The people loved him very dearly.
He dealt with everyone most fairly.
They didn't know that they were ruled.
King Arthur had his subjects fooled.

TWO BIRDS

Two birds sat upon a stone.
    One flew off, one was alone.
The other then did fly away.
    There is nothing more to say.

OLD WOMAN

There was this old Woman
and she was a shoo-in.
Children she had when
there wasn't much food in.
    She skimped and she saved
    and sent them to college.
    Feeding their minds
    with all kinds of knowledge.
This little Old Woman
was using her head.
Now, she is wealthy,
takes breakfast in bed.
    Her kids, one by one,
    found success and great wealth.
    They also remembered
    that old empty shelf.
They knew that they owed
all they had to their mother.
So they lovingly give,
each sister and brother.
    And, now, this Old Woman,
    who invested in kids,
    has pots full of money,
    she can't close the lids.
And nobody knows
that she has such great wealth.
'cause nobody checks
those pots on the shelf.

ST. IVES

As I was going to St. Ives,
    I met a man with seven wives.
"Seven wives", I heard him say,
    as he was going on his way.
I hope he can support his clan.
    He is a BRAVE and FEARLESS man.

LITTLE JACK HORNER

Little Jack Horner
    confined to a corner
        'cause he had told a lie.
           It just doesn't pay
                to get caught that way.
                    That's how he learned to be sly.

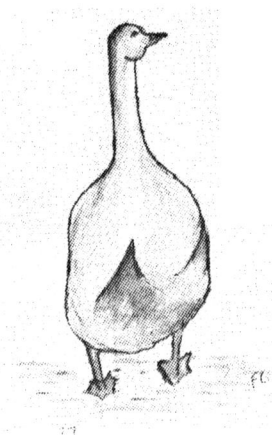

GOOSEY, GOOSEY, GANDER

Goosey, goosey, gander
where do you wander?
You waddle, waddle everywhere,
going nowhere, I declare.

On land, you don't exhibit grace
but you're magnificent in space.
You glide so smoothly on the sea.
In air you form a perfect vee.

Goosey, goosey, gander,
north and south you wander.
Uncanny is your navigation
and your timely mi-a-gration.

Goosey, goosey, gander,
you really are a wonder.
You have the very special knack
to find your nest when you come back.

TO MARKET, TO MARKET

To market, to market,
prices are down.
Industrials waver,
rails hit the ground.

> Shall I buy on the margin
> or plunge on a venture?
> I can buy on the curb
> or hold a debenture.

The market is bullish,
the market's a bear.
An open end trust
is a nice bill of fare.

> Why should I worry?
> I don't have a sou
> and I also remember,
> that the rent's coming due.

ONE MISTY MOISTY MORNING

One misty, moisty morning
  while walking on the square,
    I chanced upon a little man,
      who's hands and feet were bare.
        I turned and followed after him,
          I saw him disappear.
            The rain just seemed melt him,
              like a sugar lump, I swear.

I saw him through the misty haze.
  Nothing did distract my gaze.
    I, honestly, did see him there,
      before I saw him disappear.
        Did I imagine this whole scene?
          Could this have been an impish dream?
          My thoughts now waiver to and fro.
            It's something I shall never know.

TO BED, TO BED

"To bed, to bed," said sleepy head.
   "It's after nine, I'm off to bed."
      Fatty said, "I'll wait a little,
         I may partake of some small victual."
      Pokey said, "I'm getting wise.
         I'll stay up, won't have to rise."

So sleepy slept the whole night through
and fatty gained a little, too.
Pokey didn't have to rise,
which really didn't prove too wise.

ROCK-A-BYE BABY

Rock-a-bye baby
   on the top of a tree.
Starting in life,
   swinging dangerously.

        If the bough breaks
           and the baby falls down,
        he may hurt his psyche
        as well as his crown.

MARY HAD A LITTLE LAMB

Mary had a little lamb.
She had a problem, too.
Everywhere that Mary went
that lamb just stuck like glue.

    She had to train her pet somehow,
    this cute and cuddly little lambkin.
    Or he'd most certainly end up
    in someone's supper ramkin.

PUSSY-CAT, PUSSY CAT

"Pussy-Cat, Pussy-Cat,
where can you be?"
"I'm watching a little bird
under a tree."

"Pussy-Cat, Pussy-Cat,
what does he say?"
"I cannot convince him
I just want to play."

HI DIDDLE- DIDDLE 2

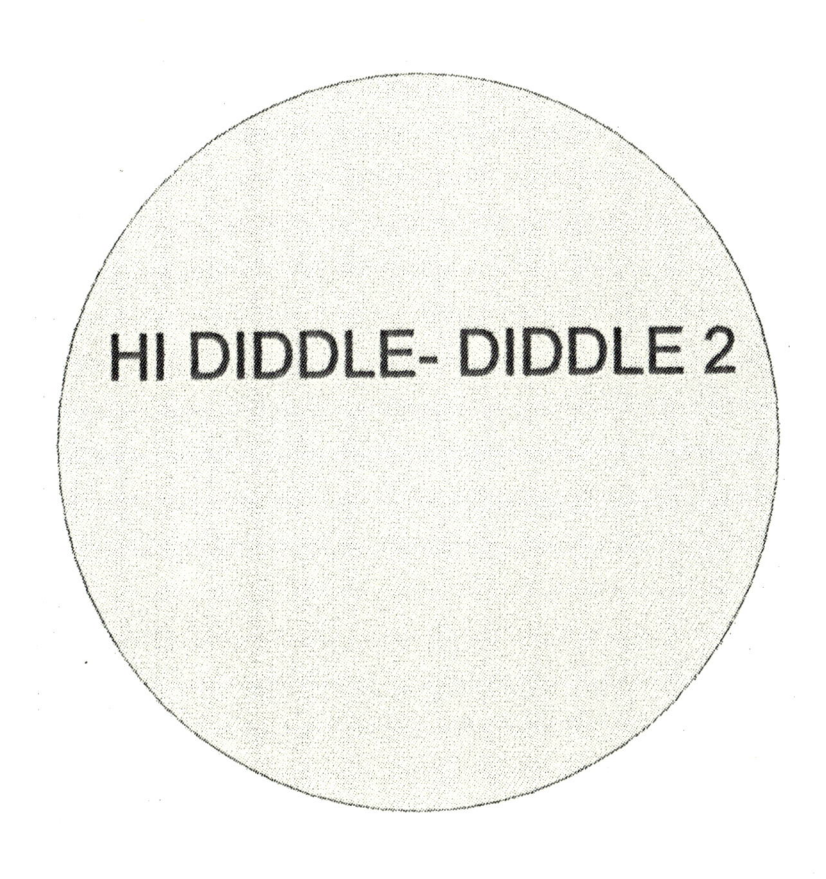

Hi Diddle-Diddle
there's no time to fiddle.
To the Moon our rocket must go.

We're lucky we made it.
Now the Russians can't take it
and charge us for Russian Moon-glow.

WEE WILLIE WINKIE

Wee Willie Winkie runs through the town.

He's improperly dressed in a flannel nightgown.

With pajamas and robe and slippers and all,

his appearance is better, he observes pro-to-col.

MARY, MARY

Mary, Mary, quite contrary,

hasn't a garden to grow.

But, flowers she gets

and it's giving her fits.

She's allergic to flowers, you know.

NORTH WIND

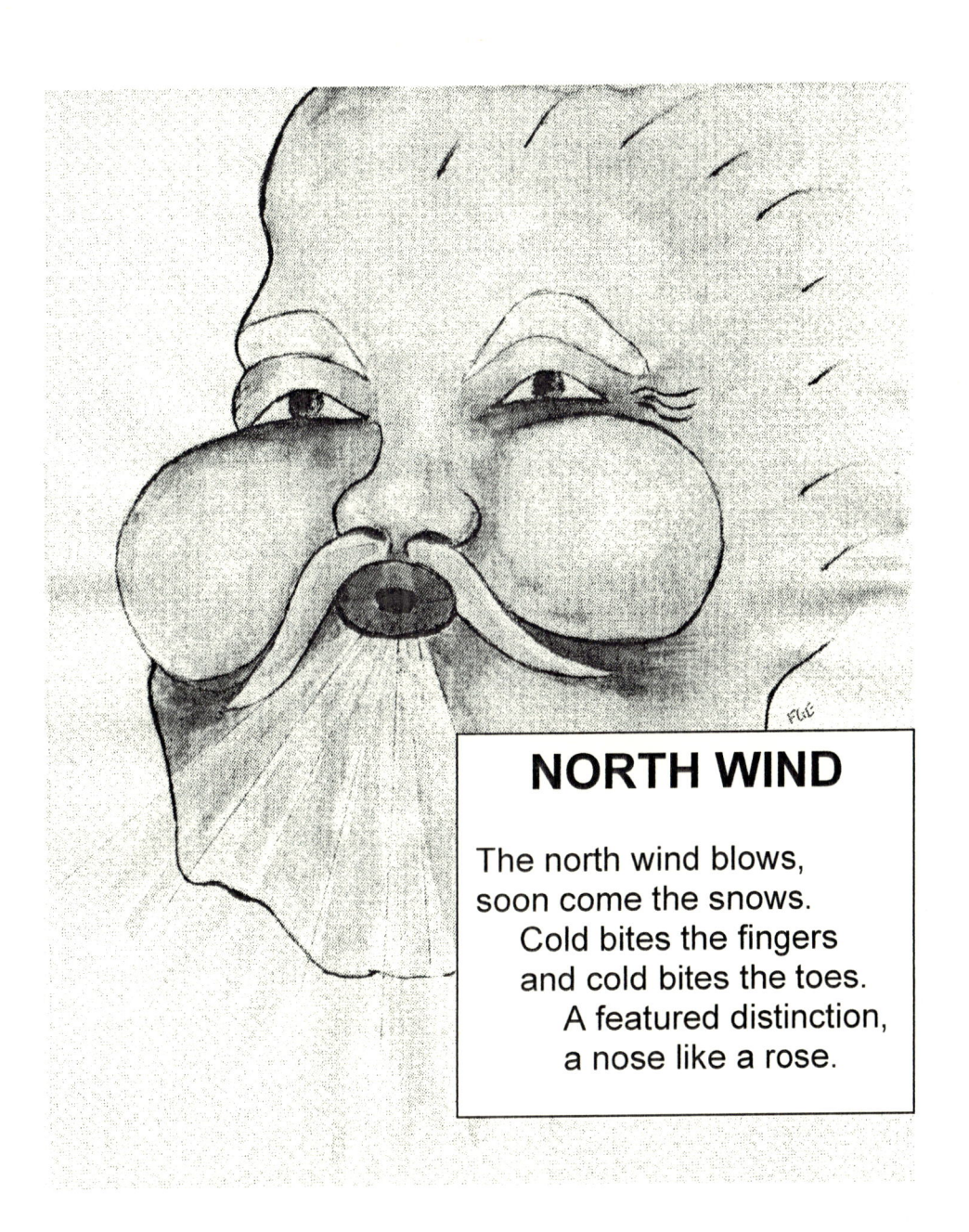

The north wind blows,
soon come the snows.
Cold bites the fingers
and cold bites the toes.
A featured distinction,
a nose like a rose.

THIS LITTLE PIG

This little pig went to market.
This little pig stayed home.
They were destined to have the very same fate,
both ending up on some gourmet's plate.

RUB-A-DUB-DUB

Rub-a-dub-dub,
  I lave and I scrub.
    And I marvel at how
      three fit in a tub.

LITTLE JACK HORNER 2

Little Jack Horner
trapped in a corner,
remembered a time-worn cliché.

With no trouble at all
he scaled the wall.
For where there's a will, there's a way.

CROSS PATCH

Cross patch, draw the latch;

don't bother to lock the door.

Who has time for a cross patch?

Friends don't come 'round anymore.

Cross patch, cross patch,

an attitude change is in store.

A grin or a smile can change your profile

and friends reappear as before.

JACK AND JILL

Jack and Jill went up the hill,
    they never made a stop.
The climbing was both hard and slow,
    at last they reached the top.

But, coming down was easy.
    It only took one slip
and they arrived post-haste below.
    It was a speedy trip.

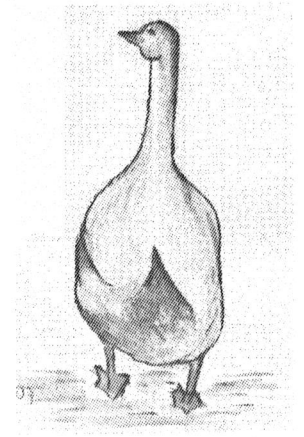

FISHY, FISHY

Fishy, fishy in the brook,
   too smart to bite upon my hook.
I will, yet, devise a plan
   to get you in my frying pan.

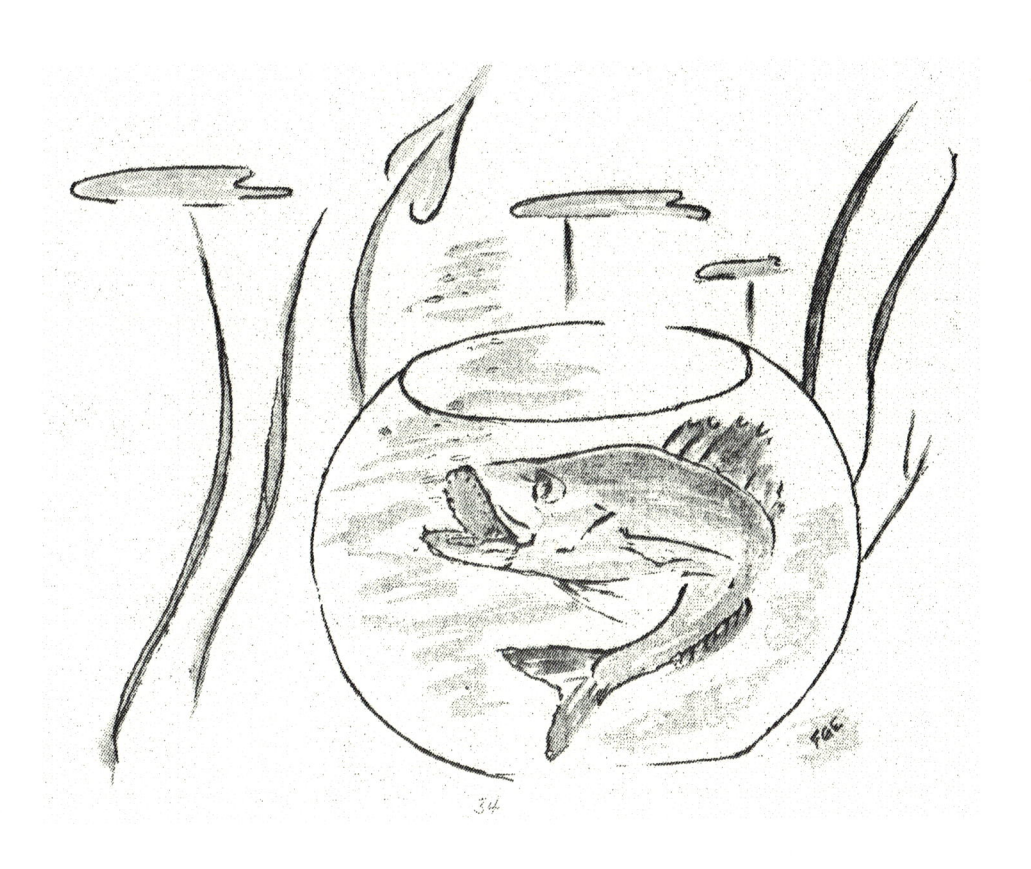

OH DEAR, OH DEAR

Oh dear, Oh dear, what can the matter be?
It's way past tea time, I haven't had my tea.
Tea and a crumpet will renew my old bounce.
Add another biscuit, I won't gain an ounce.

SEE-SAW, SEE-SAW

See-saw, see-saw, up, up to the top.
    You rise and you rise, in a moment you stop.
        Reverse the procedure and down, down you go.
        You bump at the bottom, you hit a new low.

Kind-a like life as you live it and view it.
    You hit high or low in the space of a minute.
        Life's roller coaster may give you a ride
            but somehow you manage to take it in stride.

A WISE MAN

There was a man in our town
    and he was wonderous wise.
He entered every sweepstakes
    but never won a prize.
He never seemed discouraged.
    I often wondered why?
He just sat back and said to me,
    "To win you have to try."

SING A SONG OF SIXPENCE

Sing a song of sixpence,
   I cannot tell a lie.
No matter what you've heard before,
   it was a cherry pie.

The King received it greedily
   and as he later found,
there was no more a cherry tree.
   It was hewn right to the ground.

SIMPLE SIMON 1

Simple Simon learned a lesson
   when he was very young.
He learned if you don't answer,
   you simply can't be wrong.

So Simple Simon goes through life,
   storing up his knowledge.
Though he never answers anyone,
   he's the smartest kid in college.

OLD MOTHER HUBBARD

Old Mother Hubbard
looked in the cupboard.
She found it exceedingly bare.

Her neighbors came by,
saw concern in her eye
and established a unit called "CARE".

GOD'S SPARROW

A Sparrow is so very small,
hardly anything at all.
Yet he stays in cold and snow,
facing wintry winds that blow

Every day he flies about.
He may be small but he is stout.
He has a very special way
of putting joy into each day.

TWINKLE, TWINKLE, LITTLE STAR

Twinkle, twinkle, little star,
blinking neon from afar.
Or, could you be a blinking light
of an aeroplane in flight?

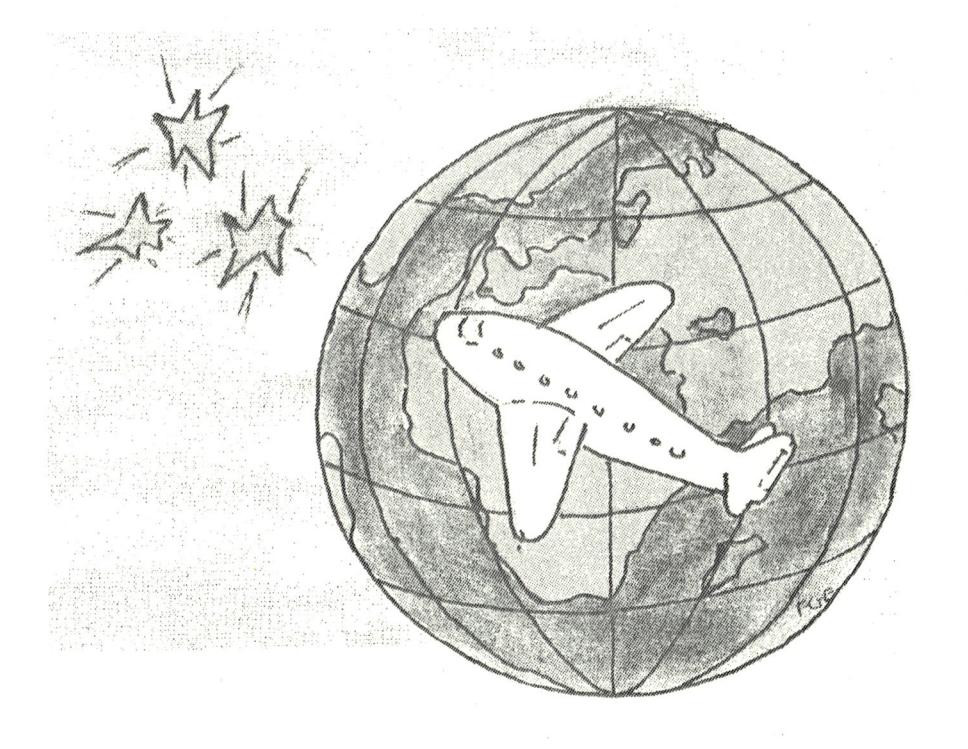

Twinkle, twinkle, star so bright,
your distance measured by years of light.
With you there is no furious race,
you're already out in space.

HUMPTY, DUMPTY

Humpty, Dumpty,
the egg on the wall,
lost his balance
and took a great fall.

The risk was more than calculated.
Too bad it had to be so ill-fated.

His fragile shell
like glass did crumble.
Humpty, Dumpty,
at last is humble.

A DILLER, A DOLLAR

A diller, a dollar,
   the people all holler
      and scream because taxes are rising.

But, with giving and lending
   and government spending,
      the stretch to a dollar's surprising.

JACK SPRAT

Jack Sprat could not eat fat
and so he fed it to his cat.

    His wife, upon the other hand,
    put all the lean in kittie's pan.

        The moral of this little ditty,
        their's is a sleek and well fed kitty.

COCK-A-DOODLE-DOO

Cock-a-doodle-doo,
    the day is breaking through.
        It's the early bird that gets the worm.
        So, I'M WAKING ME, not you.

RAIN, RAIN

Rain, rain go away,
don't rain on our parade today.
Your darkening clouds do pose a threat,
just hold your water, don't rain yet.

      If we could just negotiate
      and you would, please, cooperate,
      it would be pleasant and you'd see
      how affable we all could be.

We'll welcome you another day.
Don't give up, please, just delay.

SIMPLE SIMON - 2

Simple Simon walked about
looking for a cool handout.
Stood on corners day by day,
ambition wasn't his forté.

He walked about with hand extended.
He never seemed to be offended.
Simon was a boring jerk.
He never thought of honest work.

BIRDIE, BIRDIE

Birdie, birdie in the tree,
when you look down, what do you see?
I look up and see you soar,
'til I can't see you anymore.

You can spread your wings and fly,
your silhouette against the sky.
Here am I and here I stand
anchored to a piece of land.

Birdie, birdie in the tree,
I envy you, you envy me.

THE HANDS ON THE CLOCK

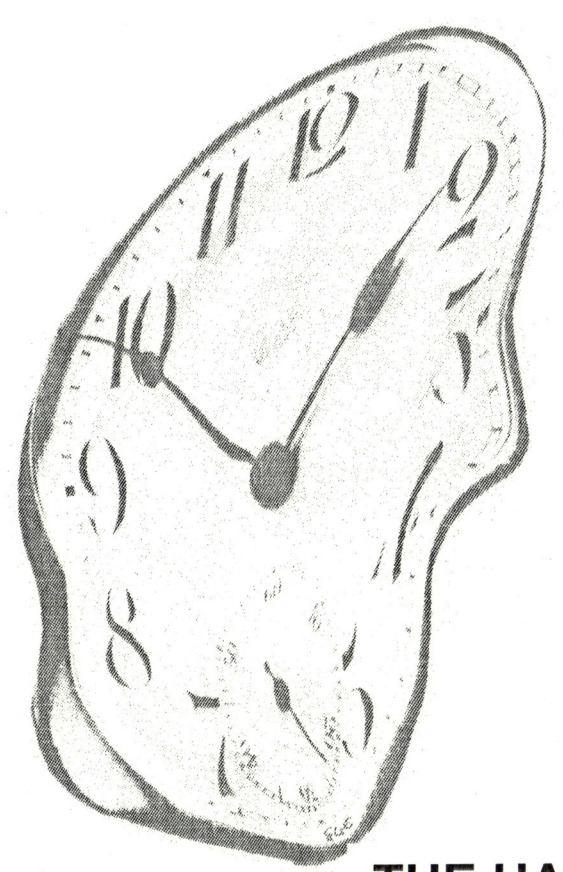

The hands on the clock, round, round they go.

Sometimes they're fast, sometimes they're slow.

It matters not to the stalwart clock.

Its major mission is a steady tick-tock.

IF WISHES WERE HORSES

If wishes were horses,
    beggars would ride.
But riding's no fun
    when you're hungry inside.

Self esteem and a job
    would be better, by far.
For a new lease on life
    trade the horse for a car.

RIP-VAN-WINKLE

Rip-Van-Winkle fell asleep.
He slept for years without a peep.

The time came when he wakened and
thought he was in a foreign land.

The world had left him far behind.
The changes nearly blew his mind.

AT NIGHT

At night, when things are dark and drear,

    it's easy to succumb to fear.

        That little tic, that twinge, that pain,

            you can't ignore, it starts again.

                Then daylight comes and you survive

                    and now it's time for nine to five.

THREE BLIND MICE

Three little mice blind as bats,
had an aversion to cats.
But danger lurks everywhere
and it's true, life's not fair.

One day they encountered a knife
and lost all their tails in the strife.
Time passes, they don't seem to mind,
now they don't have to drag them behind.

OLD KING COLE

Old King Cole was a merry old soul.

He knew and enjoyed the good life.

He was waited upon, all the day long,

and so was his merry old wife.

HICKITY, PICKITY

Hickity, pickity my black hen,
   she lays eggs for gentlemen.
      Sometimes ten and sometimes twenty.
         I'm surprised that she can lay so many.

THIRTY DAYS HAS SEPTEMBER

Thirty days has September,
　April, June and November.
　　The rest, but one, have thirty-one
　　so, when arithmetic is done,
　　　February was decreed by fate
　　　　to the remaining twenty-eight.

LADYBIRD

Once upon a time,
   there was a Ladybird.
Her husband's name was Johnson,
   of whom you've surely heard.

She didn't adopt a highway
   but she did take great pride
in beautification from coast to coast
   of the American countryside.

I SAW A SHIP A-SAILING

I saw a ship a-sailing,
   a-sailing on the sea.
It was full of treasure
   and it was all for me.

      I saw a ship a-sailing
         and then it disappeared.
      When I awakened from my dream,
         it was gone just as I feared.

CURLY LOCKS

Pretty little locks of hair,

curling here and curling there.

Brush them down and up they spring,

a shining, living, coiling thing.

A universal law should be,

curly hair by Royal Decree.

Like Camelot, a law should pass,

granting curls to every lass.

TWEEDLE-DEE-DEE AND TWEEDLE-DEE-DUM

Tweedle-dee-dee and tweedle-dee-dum

needed no reason to fight.

They quarreled and argued all the day long.

They tusseled from morning 'til night.

Should someone else get into the fray,

the table is turned and the sport has begun.

The intruder is met with resolute force.

To pummel another, instead of each other, is fun.

LADY FROM FRANCE

This chic little lady from France
    taught children and grown-ups to dance.
        She had poise and great flair,
            she displayed savoir faire.
                Her students are doing the same.
                    They follow, with pride, this great dame.

THE LION AND THE UNICORN

The Lion and the Unicorn
   had a fight to see who'd win.
  The Lion was the victor.
    Now he's the Jungle King.

SEE A PIN

See a pin and pick it up,
   or it could cause you worry.
      If you should step upon the pin,
      you'd find it in a hurry.

GOOD ADVICE

Come when you're called.

Do as I say.

Don't waste your effort,

be on time every day.

Don't worry too much.

Be good at your work.

Worry kills more, 'cause

more worry than work.

HARK, HARK

Hark, hark the dogs do bark.

There's a reason they sound an alarm.

Better attend to the ruckus they make

or you may invite bodily harm.

ALL THE SEAS

If all the seas were one sea
and there was no land around,
where would all the people be
without a spit of ground?

    All that anyone could see,
    if there was anyone around,
    a vast expanse of rolling sea
    without a spit of ground.

If this was true, a massive sea,
no lawyers there for litigation.
There'd be no thee, there'd be no me,
a shocking no-win situation.

GOOD AND EVIL

For every good,
   there is an evil.
      For every evil,
         there is a good.
            Good or evil take your pick,
               decisions must be very quick.

BYE BABY BUNTING

Bye baby bunting,

    daddy's gone a-hunting.

        I don't know what he's hunting for,

            since fur's not worn much anymore.

HUSH-A-BYE BABY

Hush-a-bye baby,
you'd better not cry.
You're fed and you're diapered,
your bottom is dry.

    Hush-a-bye baby,
    I don't know what's wrong.
    But, you have developed
    a voice that is strong.

Hush-a-bye baby,
if it's motion you need,
I'll walk you and rock you;
see, your cries did succeed.

POLLY

Polly put the kettle on
    to make some herbal tea.
        Put the cosy on the pot
            and keep it warm for me.

GIRLS AND BOYS COME OUT TO PLAY

SPRING Girls and boys come out to play,
Spring is in the air.
We're calling everyone today,
'cause the weather's mild and fair.

SUMMER Everyone come out to play,
Summer's come at last.
You'd better hurry out today,
'cause Summer passes fast.

AUTUMN Come one, come all, come out to play,
Fall has come to call.
There's not a moment to delay
or you may miss it all.

WINTER Dress warm, snow flakes gently sprinkle.
Winter always follows Fall,
or you can be like Rip-Van-Winkle,
sleep soundly and avoid it all.

ROBIN HOOD

Robin Hood and Little John
were mighty men of yore.
They would steal from the rich and famous.
The spoils ending up with the poor.

They lived in the forest primeval.
There, hidden in the glen,
they pursued their goal by day and night,
these rough and ready men.

BAA, BAA, BLACK SHEEP

Baa, Baa, Black Sheep
Straying from the fold,
pursuing wayward inclinations,
too headstrong to be told.

Baa, Baa, Black Sheep
wouldn't follow rules.
Was anti-the-establishment,
thought laws were made for fools.

Baa, Baa, Black Sheep,
the prodigal returns.
Without a friend and penniless,
with lessons still unlearned.

      The clincher

Baa, Baa, Black Sheep,
a radical change occurred.
He's now the father of a son.
The reversal seems absurd.

TEN LITTLE TOES

Ten little toes, the saying goes,

and ten little fingers, too.

Count them you'll see,

just start, "One, two, three."

Oops, there has to be more,

so count up to four.

Ten's the end of the run,

toes are all done.

Now do the fingers,

just count one by one.

If in all, there's more than twenty,
then you know, you have too many.

ABOUT THE AUTHOR

As an octogenarian I find that writing is a wonderful pastime. It exercises the brain while the rest of the body is not called upon to do anything too strenuous. Throughout my lifetime, I have had diverse experiences. I did pursue advanced education in the Arts. Later I went into aviation and became a partner in an aviation flight training school. There I learned to fly and went on to get my commercial pilot's license in light aircraft. Later we sold this business and I entered a completely different business world. I became a customer service representative for a large company. It was a challenge as I served customers in the United States and abroad. After retiring I brushed up on my writing skills by taking additional courses. With my inborn sense of humor and a love of poetry came **Another Goose Rhyme**. It was written just for the fun of it.

Printed in the United States
16655LVS00001B/58

NORMANDALE COMMUNITY COLLEGE
LIBRARY
9700 FRANCE AVENUE SOUTH
BLOOMINGTON, MN 55431-4399